05/22

$2.00

BRISTLE WITH PRIDE!

BRISTLE WITH PRIDE!

Edited by
DIRK ROBSON

illustrations by
VIC WILTSHIRE

Photographs by
COLIN ROSE

ABSON
BOOKS

Abson Books, Abson, Wick, Bristol

THE AUTHOR

After years of searching throughout five continents, literary scholars (aided by the Inland Revenue) have now abandoned all their efforts to trace the writer who hides behind the name of Dirk Robson. "Let's face it, we're stumped," said Dr Stanley Grunge, Professor of English Literature at the University of Sodding Chipbury, when he returned from a disastrous expedition up the Limpopo. "I lost half my party through malaria or litotes and all we found was a tree with 'I love Georgette Heyer' carved on it." Dr Grunge got an Arts Council grant to track down Dirk Robson, dead or alive. "The Arts Council aren't going to like this," he said, "but I don't think Dirk Robson is a person at all. I think he's a committee." Dame Phyllis Bilgewater (author of *Dirk Robson: Is He Really Lord Lucan?*) supports this view. "No one man could write all this tripe," she says. "The work is clearly an amalgam of several different types of stupidity. That explains why it still resists antibiotics." The police take a more cautious view. "We had a bloke in the cells the other day who claimed to be Dirk Robson," said a sergeant. "Or maybe it was Rob Dirkson. All them writers look alike to me." Asked what advice he would give the public if they saw anyone resembling Dirk Robson, he said: "Do not 'have a go'. He could turn out to be a committee and then you would be heavily outnumbered." The Society of Authors yesterday declined to issue a statement. "Can't help you squire, I'm not on duty, am I?" said a spokesman. "It's more than my job's worth, innit?" The quest continues in worsening conditions.

ABSON BOOKS, Abson, Wick, Bristol
First published in Great Britain, October 1987
Reprinted 1990

© Derek Robinson

Printed and bound in Great Britain by
BPCC Wheatons Ltd, Exeter

ISBN 0 902920 69 3

PREFACE

You deserve to know the truth, even if I do get flung in jail for breaking the Official Secrets Act.

The startling fact of the matter is that these three Bristle books contain the key to decoding every secret message sent by H.M. Government in the last fifty years.

Don't take my word for this. Ask someone who was in a position to know: Henry, Marquis of Strangeways (1893–1979). He joined MI5 and did so well that he was elevated to MI6, where his brilliant performance got him raised in quick succession to the dizzy heights of MI7, 8 and 9. The following afternoon he collapsed, probably suffering from oxygen starvation.

Recent reports have linked Strangeways with the KGB. This came about only because it is now known that he partnered Maclean against Burgess and Philby in the 1933 Wimbledon Men's Doubles Finals (losing in five sets, after some wild mis-hits by his partner killed two pigeons and stunned a ball-boy).

His brother, Dumbo Strangeways, still has the earl's old tennis-racquet. "I ask you," he told reporters, "does it look like a Russian spy's tennis-racquet?" This brave remark effectively silenced the critics.

Henry often preferred to communicate in Bristle, so as to baffle any foreigners from Gwent or the West Midlands who might be eaves-dropping. "Ant sinew fray jizz," he said to me when last we met. "Worse bin?"

I asked if he was still engaged in intelligence work. "Spine?" he said, and shook his head. "Stiff runt ballgame now daze. Tomb any bleed neros!"

That was when he showed me how to use the Bristle books to decode secret messages. The key is brilliantly simple. The books contain all the letters of the alphabet needed to put any word into any code. Once you know how to do that, you can quickly and easily *de*code a message by reversing the process. It's just a matter of re-arranging the letters according to a certain pattern. I could demonstrate it in a couple of minutes if I had the time.

DIRK ROBSON
Bristle
August 1987

KREK WAITER'S PEAK BRISTLE

THE AUTHOR

Dirk Robson conceals the true identity of Dr Stanley Grunge, a former professional octopus-wrestler who now occupies the Chair of Advanced Reaction at Bristle University (he keeps it in a shed at the bottom of the garden). Expelled from his Mixed Infants' School at the age of 14 for cheating at Happy Families, he stowed away on a round-the-world cruise, only emerging six months later when the ship was back where it started. In rapid succession he became a layabout, gigolo, con man, speculator, multi-millionaire, international sprinter, and mailbag-stitcher to H.M. the Queen. With maximum remission for good behaviour he made a fresh start in life as another layabout. He takes size 16 collars but wears size 14 shirts and is a martyr to splitting headaches. He lists his hobbies as reeling, writhing, and cheating the railways by taking a return and ticket not coming back. To avoid being mobbed by his admirers he invariably appears in public with his head in a brown-paper bag. As an extra precaution he wears a false moustache. The real moustache is kept in his hip pocket.

KREK WAITER'S PEAK BRISTLE

A guide to what the natives say and mean
in the heart of the Wess Vinglun

Edited by
DIRK ROBSON
who has the scars to prove it

Illustrated by
VIC WILTSHIRE

Abson Books, Abson, Wick, Bristol

FOREWORD

I have had ample opportunity to examine this book, and I am pleased to report that it is free from dysentery, croup, athlete's foot and Oregon potato blight. I also showed it to my colleague, Hercules St. John III, who is not only a distinguished epicure but also a retired police dog of considerable standing. He was unable to find any trace of cannabis resin between the pages.

Together we sampled a page, chosen at random, and it is our unanimous opinion that this book is totally indigestible. Even when grilled on toast and heavily laced with Worcester Sauce, it retains an unmistakable flavour of hydraulic brake fluid. Laboratory analysis shows this to be Duckhams Universal.

By this time it was late at night and midwinter to boot, so it seemed appropriate to test the book for combustion. Our conclusion is that it burns steadily, with a clear blue jewel-like flame and little smoke; but as a heating agent it compares poorly with *War and Peace*, the *London Telephone Directory*, and even the *Conservative Party Manifesto*.

In conclusion I can say, in all sincerity, that this book will not explode when touched with a lighted cigarette—although that, of course, could in some quarters be regarded as a drawback.

DR. LIPSBURY PINFOLD
Autopsies, Sash Cords, & 24-Hour Towing

PREFACE

I think it is important to set out clearly, right at the start, exactly what this book will not do.

It will not, for instance, help you with your income tax. (Whether it helps me with mine remains to be seen.) Nor will it improve your golf, cure your dandruff, or enlarge your biceps (unless you tear a copy to shreds every night before supper).

What it can do is solve your Christmas-card problem—not only this year, but always. Simply send this book to each of your friends, and they will never speak to you again.

Apart from that, its value is pretty limited. With the pages stapled together it makes a handy table-mat; and I have used it successfully as a wedge to stop the bedroom window rattling.

If these suggestions are no use, I can only propose that you leave it lying on top of the telly. Sooner or later your set will break down, and then you'll want something to read. Or look at the pictures. Or just sit there and hold it in your hand.

Come to think of it, that's what this book is ideally suited for: it keeps the householder company while he sits with his mouth open and his brain in neutral. Try a copy now.

Dirk Robson
Red Lun, Bristle, July 1970

KREK WAITER'S PEAK BRISTLE

Aft Trawl: Taking everything into account; as in: 'Less walk—aft trawl snot far, anna rains topped.'

Annum: Part of Bristle, near Mangusfeel. Site of Roman transit camp; hence the expression 'Per Annum', meaning 'Change at Staleton Road'.

Armchair: Question meaning 'What do they cost? 'As in: 'Armchair yer eat napples, mister?'

Avenue: Question expecting negative answer; as in: 'Avenue kids gotcher closon yet?'

Awry: Reluctant agreement: as in: 'Awry, awry, avitcherone way.'

Bart Nil: Area of Bristle between Reckliff and Lorne's ill.

Bem Breckfuss: Form of toll or tribute extorted from outsiders passing through the district. Similar to 'Overnight Accommodation', which costs 5/— more.

Bind: Not in front.

Blige: Untranslatable term, used to indicate emphasis or emotion; as in 'Blige, Bert, bleed knot, knit?'

Blow: Underneath. Opposite of **Buv.**

Bomb: The lowest level; as in: 'They mussby scrapin bomb the barrel, thassall icon say.'

Brand Nil: High point overlooking the centre of Bristle, giving good views of Bemminster, Smary Reckliff and parts of Comm, as well as the Float Narbor.

Bristle: Commercial, industrial and cultural centre of the West. Bristle has a rich social life. Two examples, chosen at random, are: *Bristle Am Chewer Pratick Sigh Tea,* and *Bristle Rovers Sporters Sigh Tea.* Others occur throughout these pages.

Butcher: Invitation to take part; as in: 'Butcher self in mice use Harry.'

Carnation: Climax of local beauty contest, as the winner gets crowned.

Claps: Fall to pieces.

Coal Snaw: Large building near the Centre of Bristle, used for wrestling and symphony concerts.

Comm: Section of Bristle between Red Lun, Snandroos and Brand Nil.

Count's Louse: Large building below Brand Nil, containing the offices of local government. Also smaller buildings inhabited by ratepayers.

Course: Musical term, e.g. *dawn course; course girl; all join in the course.*

Dan Saul: Enclosed area where deafening music is played while customers agitate themselves opposite each other. The performance may or may not be concluded with a punch-up.

Dane Age: The era in question; the way things are; as in:

'Stimey got married—aft trawl, ease twenny-sem. Snot natural' knottin this dane age.'

Deaf knit: Certain, guaranteed. As in: 'Lens a quid—lav it back Wensdee, deaf knit.'

Diesel: Introductory threat; as in: 'Diesel get my fist up thy frote.' When the fist itself is displayed, the threat may be shortened to 'Diesel getty.'

Din Chew, Din Twee: Used for questions expecting positive answers. **Din Chew** is often used aggressively, as in: 'Maida nidgetcher self genn lass night, din chew?' In contrast, **Din Twee** usually assumes total harmony; as in: 'Bert nye haddock rate big room altar selves, din twee, Bert?'

Door: Female child.

Dorne Lore: Wife of male child

Double Dover: Completely bent.

East Dregs: Highly coloured chocolate confections, eaten in the spring.

Een Pos: One of two newspapers serving Bristle and district. The other is the **Wessunday Press.** They are easily distinguishable: the **Wessunday Press** carries stories about Concorde, Bristle Docks, and luridly scandalous court cases in outlying parts of the West Country such as Kings Lynn, Glasgow and Scunthorpe; whereas the **Een Pos** carries stories about Concorde, Bristle Docks, and up to 14 solid pages of classified advertising.

Embree: Suburb of Bristle, between Lorne's Wessun and Wesbree.

Eva Narder: Patron saint of Bristle. Her name is invoked for support and encouragement whenever failure threatens, as in:

17

'Snow good give nup—try Eva Narder.' Also: 'They played hard, but we played Eva Narder.'

Fax: Data.

Fee: Opening of suggestion, as in : 'Fee cries, gimmis boll.' Similar openings are **Fie, Few** and **Fitz,** as in :

> 'Fie scene, I'll punchiz teefin.'
> 'Few wannum, better pay forum.'
> 'Fitz wet, I'm stain omen watchin telly.'

Fight Old Jew: Hint of remarkable revelations ; as in : 'Fight old jew hooey stake nowt, ewed beam azed.'

Flat List: Stamp collector.

Forced Dean: Large wooded area in Gloucestershire.

Ford: Opposite of backward.

Foreign: With another person in mind ; as in : 'Ussle wait foreign ear.'

Furze: To an extent ; as in : 'Saul overrun dunwith, furze icon see.

Genny; Gonny: These interchangeable words are widely used to introduce an inquiry concerning the availability of items or objects. **Genny** is used where a third party has been involved in the transaction ; e.g. 'Genny good books uppa lye bree ?' On the other hand, **Gonny** is used for direct questioning : 'Gonny thin teat ? Gonny threench nails ? Gonny sisters tome ?'

Geronwy: See **Stain.**

Gloss Trode: Shopping area and highway leading north out of Bristle.

Gorgeous: Inevitable remark by visitors to Clifton, as in : 'The gorgeous bewful, innit ?'

Grace Tepp-Ford: Bristle's First Lady, and an essential figure in all public works. Her name is hailed to justify spending the

ratepayers' money on everything from bigger roundabouts (distributing the traffic jams so that everybody gets a bit) to computerised crematoria (despatching us to eternity with split-second efficiency). Hardly a municipal speech goes by without some reference to her: 'Before declaring this Sewage Treatment Works open, I should like to congratulate the citizens of Bristle on another Grace Tepp-Ford.'

In her time, Mrs Tepp-Ford has been associated with many notable events in Bristle. The Brabazon was a Grace Tepp-Ford. Broadmead shopping centre was a Grace Tepp-Ford. There was a report that the recent modernisation and improvement of the Bristle bus services was yet another Grace Tepp-Ford, and judging by the number of people to be seen walking home, that's probably right.

Grain: Turning grey.
Grout: See **Less.**

Hard Tack: Cardiac failure.
Honest Ale: Close behind. Police jargon, frequently used in *Softly, Softly:* 'Keep honest ale, Barlow. Watchim Leica nawk.'

Incher: Challenge; as in: 'Drinkin my scrumpy, incher?'
Intense: Under canvas.

Jeer: This is one of two words widely used in conversation to draw attention to items of news. **Jeer** refersto news transmitted by the spoken word. An example of its use is:
'Jeer onna news poster rain all necks munf?'
'Jeer bout Stan come nup onna Pools? Won semmen forms.'

21

'Jeer er-necks-door go non bout R bonfire downa bomba garn? Sedditz smoky nupper washin.'

For reference to news transmitted visually, see **Sauna.**

Jew Asbestos: Expression of disbelief; as in: 'Jew asbestos bleev that?'

Justice Swell: Expression of right and proper behaviour; as in: 'No, we dingo way, we stay dome. Justice swell—trained all week.'

Knee: Key to general enquiry; as in: 'See knee M.T. cease?' 'Bring knee thin treed?'

Krek: Accurate; as in: 'Krek time squaw pass sen.'

Kwor: Four ounces.

Lav: Note of urgency or compulsion; as in: 'Lav turry—slate.' 'Lav towarder writ, luv, snottin stock.'

Lay Tron: In due course; as in: 'Sid seddy might poppin lay tron. Stimey did—ease eddied beer yes-day.'

Less: Proposal of action; as in: 'swarm near, knit? Less grout.' Or: 'Less bailey tout—scotta lotta wart rinse ide.'

Lorne's ill: District of Bristle situated in Up Reaston. It lies between Bart Nil, Staleton Road, and the Riv Raven.

Mangus Feel: Rural community to the north-east of Bristle.

Mansh Nowce: Lord Mayor's residence.

Miniature: The very instant; no sooner than; as in: 'Miniature back sterned, summonse upto summit.'

Mince: Short periods of time. See also **Munce.**

Moff: Statement of departure; as in: 'Moff to Scouse now, dad–connive me pock-money?'

Moira Wave Life: Whenever the citizens of Bristle find the plain, unvarnished truth a bit of a strain on the eyeballs, they call in Moira Wave-Life to refurbish the facts and create a more glamorous image. Miss Wave-Life runs a Public Relations agency which is so successful that the very sound of her name is enough to transform the dullest activity into an exciting, rewarding crusade. 'Pickled eggs,' declares a typical press release from her agency, 'are not so much an industry—Moira Wave-Life.'

Munce: Long periods of time. See also **Mince.**

Muse Call: Old-fashioned entertainment, killed off by telly, which in turn is so terrible that old-fashioned Muse Call has now been revived, in places.

Myrrh: Looking-glass.

Natchafack: To tell the truth; in reality; as in: 'Saul lies, yerronner! Natchafack I nev reeven touch dim—he mustard riven into a waller summit.'

Ness Serry: What's needed. Anything that's tzar bull but not absolutely sensual is ness serry.

Nev Reeven: See **Natchafack.**

Nigh: Plaintive ending of defensive statement; as in: 'Av nart—I'm doona bess-eye can, nigh?' 'Woss speck—I only got one pair vands, nigh?'

Nurse Gnome: Kind of high-class hospital. Good place to recover from a claps.

On Slee: Actually; in truth. Often used for emphasis, with a l thrown in for good measure; as in: 'So I said, "Lissen," I said, "woss mean?" I said. Annie sediment watty said, from the

bomb is art. On slee!'

Pain Guess: Long-term boarder.

Payment: Sidewalk; as in: 'Stain a payment—you'll get knock dover.'

Phoney: Wishful thinking; as in:
- A. 'Phoney I cud grow brockley biggs yorn, Bert. Woss put on un?'
- B. 'Scald "The Mixture", Sid. Wife gessit frommer doctor. Dunt doer chess knee good, but it dough-naff bring on my brockley, loik.'

Plain: Taking part in organised sport; as in:
- Q. "Wisey plain sent-raff?'
- A. 'Avenue erred? Reggler sent-raffs busty sand.'

Plain Feels: Sports grounds.

Pine Chips: Popular meal with café society. Others include Scramble Decks and Saucy Jeggan Chips.

Port Zed: Coastal town opposite Avemouth. The Macao of the West.

Ree's Knees: Explanation; as in: 'Ree's knees fed up scuzzies onny zone, C.'

Reporse: Newspaper stories.

Rifle: Deserving. Prince Charles is the Rifle Air.

Sane: Expression, proverb; as in Old Country Sane, and Sane of the Week.

Sartnoon: Later on today.

Sauna: Word used extensively in conversation to draw attention to items of news. **Sauna** refers to news transmitted in pictures; for instance:

'Sauna telly lass night bout all them forced fires nosstralia. 'Sauna news they got jam surround X-ter gain. Sauls the same, knit?'

See also **Jeer**.

Scars: Cylinders of tobacco, reputedly a damn good smoke.

Scold: Evidence of the white-hot pace of intellectual ferment in Bristle is the ability of its citizens to use only one word to communicate complex ideas which require several words elsewhere in the country. **Scold** (the weather is not as warm as it might be) is an example. Others are:

Scum (It has arrived.)

Slate (It has not arrived.)

Snot (I am afraid you have miscalculated.)

Snow? (Are you aware of what I have revealed to you?)

Snuff (That is quite sufficient.)

Surly (It has arrived ahead of time.)

Swarm near (This room is noticeably hot.)

Stun (The project has been completed.)

You will see from this list that it is possible in Bristle to conduct a valuable exchange of views while using only a handful of words. Here are two Bristolians discussing the End of the World:

A. Scum!

B. Snot, snow. Slate.

A. No, scum. Surly. Sought meself.

B. (Furiously) Snot! Snot! Slate!

A. (Curiously) Smatter?

B. (Brokenly) Snout . . . Swarm near . . . (Whispering) Sure scum?

A. Scum, awry. Saul over. (PAUSE) Scold out.

B. Swarm near, though. Snuff, knit?

A. Snuff? Sample! (PAUSE, THEN QUIETLY:) Scum. On slee.

B. (SIGHS HEAVILY) Stun . . .

Seedy: Much of the rich fabric of life in Bristle is the result of constant contact—people recognising each other, and recognising that they themselves have, in turn, been recognised. The codeword **Seedy** is invaluable for this exchange, and it is heavily used. For instance:

A. Seedy uppa Rovers, Sat-dee.

B. Ah? Dint C.D., though. Whirr bouts wast?

A. Bind a goal.

B. Oh, ah. Yer, seedy gotten gaged, den! Zinna paper wonnit?

A. R. Genn marred up Smarys, prolly.

Sensual: Vital, crucial; as in: 'Snot juss ness serry—sab slootly sensual.' See also **Ness Serry.**

Shleedown: Residential area of Bristle, near Snandroos.

Shrampton: Another residential area of Bristle, between Lorne's Wessun and Avemouth.

Sill Sernt: Government employee.

Sin: Not standing. Sin room: place where tea is served on Sundays.

Skewer Tea: Freedom from anxiety; confidence; as in: 'Pay saul right, butties got no skewer tea.'

Snandroos: Part of Bristle, not far from Red Lun.

Snanz: Another part of Bristle, between Lorne's ill and Annum. It lies in a bend of the Riv Raven.

Smary Reckliff: What visitors mistake for Bristle Cathedral.

Sporse: Organised games, usually conducted on plain feels

People who attend sporse but don't take part are known as **Sporters**.

Sporse Scar: Loud and uncomfortable means of transportation. Usually does 12 miles to the gallon. Insurance premiums for sporse scars are calculated by multiplying the maximum speed by 2 and adding 50 if the driver is an actor, a student, a professional sporseman, or under 65.

Stain: Don't go out; as in: 'Moff to bingo—yew stain Geronwy yer Romework.'

Star Craven Mad: Mildly eccentric if rich. Dangerously irresponsible if poor.

Summer Thurr: More or less in that direction.

Sunny's Cool: Bible class for the young.

Stay Plill: District of Bristle, on the way to Mangus Feel.

Stiff Cut: Diploma.

Tessa Strenff: Conflict and strife seldom raise their ugly heads in Bristle, but when they do we have a champion worthy of the occasion. Tessa Strenff has appeared so often that it is impossible to imagine a strike, a demonstration, or a municipal squabble being reported without her aid. "The whole dispute," we have been told, time and time again, "has turned into a Tessa Strenff." After that the reporter gets bogged down in a lot of boring detail which we can safely ignore, knowing that as long as Tessa's on the scene nobody is likely to chicken out.

Tree member: To bear in mind; as in: 'Few loss tit, sup chew to fine dit. Wear javit lass? Try tree member!'

Truss: Faith, confidence. Also used of charitable bodies, e.g. National Truss.

Tuthrend: Down thurr, not up yer.

Tzar Bull: Attractive; worth having but not at any price. See also **Ness Serry** and **Sensual**.

Waddle: Request for advice; as in: 'Waddle-eye do? Scone midnight anny snot tome yet. Sun-like R Tom, stain out slates this.'

War: Basic commodity, supplied by Bristle War Works. Unless heated, it is coal war.

Wessun: Bristle's answer to Majorca.

Wess Vinglun: The region around Bristle. Many regional organisations have their headquarters in Bristle, e.g. Wess Vinglun Colge Vart.

Wimms Inns Toot: Militant female movement dedicated to fighting pollution, making jam, wearing hats, and singing Jerusalem'.

Wive Alley: Course of river separating England from Wales.

Woot Nun Dredge: Pleasant village at present to the north of Bristle, doomed one day to be absorbed by the city's sprawl unless somebody puts his foot down.

Wreck Knits: The act of estimating or calculating; as in:
Motorist: Sport Zed long yer, den?
Pedestrian: R. Wreck knits bout mile naff, stray ted.

Y Tree: Notorious roundabout between Red Lun and Wesbree.

Yearn: Two meanings, (1) As part of the phrase 'Yearn Thurr' meaning 'scattered about.'
(2) By itself, meaning 'the ability to hear'; as in 'Lav to shout—ease ardour yearn.'

Yerp: The Continent.

SON OF BRISTLE

SON OF BRISTLE

A second guide to what the natives say and mean
in the heart of the Wess Vinglun

Edited by
DIRK ROBSON
using an old garden-rake

and illustrated by
VIC WILTSHIRE
wielding a sharp knife and fork

Abson Books Abson Wick Bristol

For my mother
(*who always keeps her guid Scots accent*)

ACKNOWLEDGEMENTS

Nobody helped me compile this book; I did it all myself, except for the pictures which Vic Wiltshire drew (brilliantly).

In particular, I got no help from SWEB, who supply such feeble power to this part of Bristle that even my chilblains got frostbite last winter; from the Inland Revenue, who persist on taxing me on the money I haven't yet made as well as on the money I've already spent; from the licensing laws, which make me drink when I'm not thirsty and leave me thirsty when I need a drink; from the pigeons in the attic overhead, who play football and perform clog-dances while I'm trying to work; from the kids next door, who keep waking me up while I'm pretending to think; from Bill Fry, who declines to let me beat him at squash; and above all from J. Grimsby Fish, who ratted on me after I had given him five bob as agreed.

FOREWORD

I am delighted to recommend this useful little book, because the author has promised to pay me if I do—not much money, to be sure, but then it's not much of a book and besides, I'm not much of a recommendation.

In fact, when you get right down to it, I suppose neither the book nor myself is really worth a fraction of the amounts involved. What's more, if any of us had a scrap of decency or an ounce of honesty in our decadent, crumbling bodies we would never allow ourselves to get involved in such a lousy, crumby little deal as this.

My God! They must think I've fallen pretty low if they expect me to risk my reputation over their cheap bit of catchpenny trash, all for a mere pittance! Listen here, Robson, you bum—I wouldn't tout your tatty pamphlets for you if you gave me a thousand quid, d'you hear that?

What d'you think I am, some sort of cheap hypocrite? Get lost, and take your garbage with you. I have never read your grubby little book, but I know one thing for sure. It stinks. (And you can quote me on that.)

J. GRIMSBY FISH
Divorce Enquiries
Lawnmowers Ground and Set
Private Tap-Dance Lessons

THE AUTHOR

For many years it was thought that Dirk Robson concealed the true identity of Dr Stanley Grunge, a former professional octopus-wrestler who was given the Chair of Advanced Reaction at Bristle University after he had loudly admired it at a party. However, the untimely loss of Dr Grunge (found sprawled on his library floor with a ghastly expression on his face and a pickled onion stuffed up each nostril) made it necessary to reconsider this view; and it is now thought likely that Dirk Robson is really Lady Flossy Strop-Fetlock, the only woman on record who has kicked a Rugby ball across the Thames while holding a glass of sherry in each hand. She is also the only woman known to have addressed the Dutch Parliament in fluent Burmese, and vice versa. Lady Flossy has been married seven times, five of them to the bandleader Dudley Trubshaw and twice to a completely different Dudley Trubshaw whom she mistook for the bandleader because it was so dark at the time. She has a size-6 foot and wears size-4 shoes which hurt incessantly. She rarely appears in public, because people often mistake her for the *other* Flossy Strop-Fetlock (the one who feeds her begonias on scrambled egg, and then sings); and this she finds awfully sad, somehow.

PREFACE

This book is a sequel to 'Krek Waiter's Peak Bristle'. Behind them both lies a curious story.

When 'Krek Waiter's Peak Bristle' first came out, several bookshops stocked it under the impression that it was a Greek phrase-book for tourists, and many customers bought it under the impression that it was a load of old rubbish (but cheap at the price).

Startled by this success, the publishers blew the profits on a long weekend at Severn Beach. They got back to find on the doormat a demand note from the Inland Revenue. Searching the premises for something to pawn, they came across three tons of plain paper in the billiard room. It was lightly mildewed at the edges but still quite firm in the centre.

An hour later I received a telegram: PLEASE WRITE SMALL CHEAP BESTSELLER STOP NO PORN STOP DON'T JUST SIT THERE WITH YOUR MOUTH OPEN GET CRACKING STOP.

The result was 'Son of Bristle'. Many people did their best to discourage me. "For God's sake, no," wrote the Bishop of Peebles. "Haven't you done enough damage already?" demanded Dame Flora Couchgrass, the vegetarian and former roller-skate sprint champion. "Just watch it," warned Dudley Grunge (24) of Slough.

Outright intimidation followed. Hostile women jostled me at

jumble sales, and I was savagely hacked on the shins while playing Rugby. The roof of my car was repeatedly fouled by trained pigeons, some probably Communists.

Nevertheless, 'Son of Bristle' was completed, and here it is—a load of brand-new rubbish, but still cheap at the price.

Dirk Robson
Red Lun, Bristle, July 1971

EUREKAL! The famous Bristle L

Bristle is the only city in Britain to be able to turn ideas into ideals, areas into aerials, and Monicas into monocles.

Nobody knows why the Bristle folk slap an L on the end of any and every word which offers a conveniently overhanging 'a' or 'o' sound, but they do, and it's been going on for a long time. 'Bristle' itself was made out of *brig* (bridge) and *stowe* (place) plus a final L to keep the dust out.

Probably the most famous result of the Bristle L was the city father who had three lovely daughters, Idle, Evil and Normal. (To these can be added three other uniquely Bristle girls: Annal, Martial and Monocle.) But without a doubt the most telling demonstration of the Bristle L took place a couple of years ago when a television crew recorded several citizens while they read aloud the words on a theatre poster, which turned out to be featuring Eval Turner, Primal Donnal of the Carl Rosal Operal. It goes without saying that the company performed such works as Aidal, La Traviatal, Rigolettol, and Cavaleria! Rusticanal.

Few foreign countries are safe from the Bristle L. It ranges the world, from Nigerial to Malaysial, from Bolivial to Australial, from Costal Rical to the Costal Braval. It affects Canadal and Americal (for which you need a visal) as well as the notorious malarial areal of Africal.

But it is in everyday life that the Bristle L flourishes. A local girl who was learning to dance was heard to say, "I can rumble but I can't tangle." Bristle housewives go shopping for bananals, semolinal, tinned tunal fish, and a Victorial sandwich, as well as Ryvital and Ambrosial creamed rice. Kitchen tops are covered with Formical. Sinks are cleaned with ammonial.

Hardly anything in the garden escapes—begonials, fuschials, dahlials, hydrangeals, even aspidistrals. And not even diseases are immune. People in Bristle have been struck down by the grisly influenzal and pneumonial. Happily, diphtherial is rare, although visitors should beware the dreaded Dire Eel.

Neither television nor religion offers any escape from the Bristle L. You're just as likely to find yourself watching Panoramal, or a programme from Granadal, or a re-run of the Forsyte Sagal; and if you go to church it will probably turn out to be either St Teresal's, St Helenal's, St Brendal's or St Kildal's.

You can always get in your car and drive away, of course. Just make sure it isn't a Cortinal, Anglial, Simcal, Lancial, Hondal, Toyotal, Alfal-Romeol, Vival, Volvol, etceteral, etceteral, etceteral.

SON OF BRISTLE

Annuity: Claim to insight; as in: 'Annuity was line, cuzzy turn dread.'

Ant Eye: Appeal for support, usually tacked on to end of sentence; as in: 'Core sigh can't goat the pitchers. Gotta state tome an mine the baby, ant eye?'

Am Rim: Cry uttered by spectators at Rugby match whenever opponent gets the ball.

Ashen Core: Former stately home, still standing in rolling parkland near Long Ashen.

Beers Port: Ancient chant, traditionally uttered by the natives in order to bring about a change of fortune. Rarely successful.

Beet Root Chew: Declaration of faithfulness; as in: 'I'll always beet root chew, luv.'

Bit Rend: Unpleasant outcome.

Bren Jam: Popular food item.

Bristle Grams Cool: Local academy for boys.

Buffer: Had circumstances been otherwise; as in: 'Buffer rim, she'd bean side a nurse gnome now.'

Bum Tinto: Met by chance; as in: 'Guess why bum tinto in Shrampton smorning?'

Butt Knoll: Small slit in clothing.

Canteen: Measure of extreme inability; as in: 'Fat? He canteen seize zone feet knee more!'

Carnival: Warning against greed; as in: 'Yer, you carnival them straw breeze!'

Cease: Chairs.

Cess Rees: Extra items, e.g. gloves, handbags, earrings, etc. Sometimes known as 'Matchin Cess Rees', which cost 25% more.

Chess: Upper part of body, e.g. Chess Eggs Ray.

Clift Nice Cool: Bristle's answer to Roedean.

Clyde: Run into.

Corsairs; Corsets: These words usually introduce a confident claim, such as: 'Corsairs moron one waiters kin a cat.' Or: 'Corsets knotter real usban, juno.'

Deck Rating: Painting and wallpapering.

Dennis: Tooth doctor.

Dummy: Phrase meaning 'completed my'; as in: 'Tell meal laughter wait—I can't seam till eye dummy pools.'

Dwight Elm Outer: Start of retaliatory remark tinged with indignation; as in: 'Wine tea mined zone business? Aft trawl, dwight elm outer do *is* job?'

Earner: Expression of feminine contempt; as in: 'Ooze she kidding wither big eye deals? Earner count's louse!'

Ev Smuch: A great deal, a lot. **Ev S'** is the universal term of emphasis in Bristle. For example, 'Ev Sgood' means anything from 'not bad' to 'fantastic'. Other Ev-words are: Ev Snice, Ev Seasy, Ev Soften, Ev Sot, Ev Scold, Ev Sweat, Ev Slate, Ev Sold and Ev Sevvy.

Fairy Nuff: Expression of satisfaction, based on the wellknown passion of the Little Folk for British justice. (For the benefit of those unfamiliar with the world of elves and pixies, Fairy Nuff was the one in Enid Blyton with red hair and freckles, who was victimised when Noddy circulated false rumours of drunkenness and shoplifting and had her hounded out of the Union. It was in all the papers.)

Feud: Beginning of suggestion; as in: 'Feud shrup a mint, you'd seat eye mean.' A similar opening is **Fuel;** as in: 'Fuel grout an shove, I'll stain side and steer.'

Fig Red: Statue at sharp end of ship.

Finch: End; as in: 'Ant chew finched yet?'

Fine: Discover.

Fought: Considered.

Four Stout: Ejected by force; as in this typical piece of Rugby commentary: '. . . annie nearly scores butties four stout . . .'

Freeze A Bird: Completely at liberty.

Ginger: Start of question concerning wellbeing; as in:
    A. 'Scold out smornin—Ice lipped onna payment.'
    B. 'Ginger yourself?'

Gnat Case: In those circumstances.

Gnome: Claim acquaintance with; as in: 'Gnome? Coarse eye gnome! We bin mace for munce!'

Grape Ride: Much self-esteem.

Grape Written: England, Ireland, Scotland and Wales. The **S.S. Grape Written** is in dry dock in Bristle.

Greyful: Appreciative. **Moron Greyful:** Highly appreciative.

Groan Pains: Childhood discomfort.

Gross Rees: Household goods sold in, e.g. supermarket.

Guard Nose: Horticultural equipment.

Guess Tuck Interim: Advice uttered by spectators at football match, esp. when player appears reluctant to engage whole-heartedly in the action.

Guise: (see **Scouse.**)

Ice Pecked: Suggest a likelihood; as in: 'Ice pecked ease gone infra beer.'

Ice Pose; Ice Poseys; Ice Poser: Suggest a possibility, as in: 'Snot on telly, ice pose?'
'Ice poseys gone wafer is oll daze.'
'Ice poser dad wooden letter seam again.'

Instant: Happening, event.

Into: Not very; as in: 'She into good at sums, butter jogger fee slot better.'

Isolate: Indicates reluctance to act; as in: 'Isolate moon away from Bristle. Aft trawl, swear I grup, innit?'

Jubilee: Question of opinion; as in: 'Jubilee view should stake wyatt? Or jubilee vince pekin your mine?'

Juicy: Word used to introduce an inquiry about something taking place; as in:

'Juicy what icy?'

or 'Juicy the nude reins bean laid inna necks treat?'

Lady Slavs: Half of a public convenience.

Lass Mint: Very late; urgent.

Lay Bricks Change: Department of Employment.

Lean Tomb: Recommendation of non-interference; as in: 'Yer! You lean tomb self, rile beacher red in!' A similar phrase is **Lean Lone;** as in: 'That paint sweat—lean lone!'

Lecher: Permissive advice; as in: 'Wine chew guess tuck inter the scrumpy, an lecher rare down?'

Lessee: Note of caution; as in:

    A. Started train—we might swell goat the pitchers.

    B. Well, lessee fits gonny buddy good knit, first.

Libel: Likely or inclined; as in: 'Coal Snaw's libel to be soul doubt.'

Lice: Illuminations. These take many forms, such as Head Lice (on cars) and Street Lice (in public places).

Lice Witch: Device for controlling lice. However, a **Lice Plit** is an alcoholic beverage.

Line: Dishonest; as in: 'Ease line, yeronner!'

Log Reds: Deadlock.

Lonely Bee: Understatement; as in:

'Yukon stain a car few like—lonely bee fie mince.'

or: 'Jew wanna comfortee? It lonely bee bren jam, ice pecked.

Loss: Large quantities; plenty.

McNubbout: Many words owe their origins to surnames. 'Hooligan' came from a delinquent Irish family in London, the

57

O'Hulihans. The Earl of Sandwich invented the packed lunch, Wellington gave us the boot, and it was a Brighton greengrocer (and amateur inventor) by the name of W. C. Flush who perfected the modern toilet; while we owe the word 'harass' to a notoriously persistent rent-collector in 18th-century Lancashire, one Zebedee Harris.

Bristle's contribution to this list comes from a Scottish kilt-manufacturer, Hamish McNubbout (1753–1829) who came south and established a business in Reckliff. Demand for kilts in that part of Bristle was slight, and Hamish McNubbout found himself with so much time on his hands that eventually his name became a byword for idling. When asked by their parents what they had been up to, kids used to mumble: 'Juss McNubbout.' In those days they usually got a clip on the ear for not speaking properly.

Major: Reflection on some other person's behaviour, as in: 'Ant chew major mine dup yet?'

Mill: Centre.

Mine: Intellect.

Mine Jew: Take into account.

Neck Store: Neighbouring.

Neuter: Unfamiliar with; as in:
  A. 'How dye getta Gloss Trode?'
  B. 'Dunno, I'm neuter Bristle.'

Nice Cool: Evening institute.

Nose Snot: Negative reply; as in:
  A. Din ronna table yet?
  B. Nose snot.

Office Ed: Daft. The original Office Ed was a clerk named Edward Upjohn, who worked in a Chinese spaghetti factory in Bemmister. People used to get drunk and telephone him in the middle of the night, saying: 'Are you up, John?' It drove him daft.

Oliver Sun: Unexpectedly.

Ooze Pain: Query about source of money.

Pasture: This way; as in: 'Scene knee numb rate buses go pasture?'

Plea Scar: Panda.

Plover: Kind of sweater.

Prayed: March-past.

Ray-Joe Bristle: Local broadcasting station with two DJ's Ray Gin-Eddake and Joe Kinnapart.

Relay: Emphatic response indicating mild astonishment; as in:
  A. 'Ant chew erred? Easy loped wither from neck store!'
  B. 'No! Relay?'

Rival: Entry.

Rub Sheep: Pile of garbage.

Scampi: Statement of impossibility; as in: 'This scampi wary lives—scot no lice on.'

Scene Sow: Under the prevailing conditions; as in: 'Scene sow ease always onna beer, snow under he puss on smuch weight.'

Scouse: (see **Guise.**)

Seizure: It's not so difficult; as in: 'One shoe guess tarted, seizure knit looks.'

61

Senior: Start of personal enquiry; as in: 'Senior dad knee wear? Ease poster mimi yer quart van our ago.'

Serfs: The outside area.

Shane Cream; Shane Soap: Male toiletries.

Short Urn: You're next.

Sickle Downer: Nauseated; as in: 'R Normal went honour Sunny's Cool out-in yesdee, and she was sickle downer teacher's plover.'

Sikh Debts: Teenage sailors.

Skills: Pub game.

Smite Urn: I'm next.

Snow Under: I'm not surprised.

Sordid Doubt: Cleared up, explained; as in: 'Saul micks tup—summoned better sordid doubt.'

Sparky: Snot ott.

Stans Treason: Commonsense indicates.

Story Cheaters: Way of keeping the house warm.

Stray Ford: Simple, honest, uncomplicated.

Strew: That's right.

Sum Set: Neighbouring county.

Sup Chew Knit: Passing the buck. For example:
  A. 'Waddle eye sate rim, fee guess fresher summit?'
  B. 'Sup chew, knit?'

Tale Tense: Ping-pong.

Tall Deep Ends: Praps. On the other hand, praps not.

Tour Free: Less than 4.

Toes Track: Device for keeping burnt bread cold at breakfast.

Waddle Eye Sate: see **Sup Chew Knit**.

Wafer: see **Ice Poseys.**

Wane: Entrance.

Wine Tea: see **Dwight Elm Outer.**

Wodge: Opening word of cross-examination; as in: 'Wodge you mean bite?'

Word: Anxious.

Work Knee; Work Nigh: Enquiries concerning whereabouts; for example:

'Work knee parky scar?'

'Work nigh see the prayed?'

Worm Stew: Further enquiry concerning whereabouts; for example:

    A. 'Pretty ice lated yer, incher? Worms stew gopher yer gross rees?'

    B. 'Bout mile naff, ice pose. Mine jew, the misses bake slot.

Wreck Ross: International disaster-relief agency.

Yule Laughter: Opening words of command or requirement; as in: 'Yule laughter buyer summit—aft trawl, sir birthday.' See also **Dummy.**

Yuma: Lead-in to descriptive remark, such as:

'Yuma secker tree yer, incher?'

or: 'Yuma lines wine!'

BRISTLE RIDES AGAIN

For Maurice Webster

BRISTLE RIDES AGAIN

A third guide to what the natives say and mean
in the heart of the Wess Vinglun

Edited by
DIRK ROBSON
using a reconditioned vacuum cleaner

with photographs by
COLLIE N'ROSE
wearing Lord Snowdon's old pullover

Abson Books, Abson, Wick, Bristol

ACKNOWLEDGEMENTS

To Daguerre for inventing photography, to Eastman for inventing the roll film, and to Kodak for inventing the modern camera. To Gutenberg for inventing printing, and to Caxton for swiping it and bringing it to England. To Sheila for inventing food (several times) and to Samuel Whitbread and Arthur Guinness for inventing lubricating fluids. And finally to Chris Denham and Julian Dunne, for standing under the bubbles next to the statue of the soldier, and while the pubs were open, too.

FOREWORD

I have known the author for so many years — he was my batman during the Battle of Jutland, or it may have been the other way around — that I feel entitled to suggest one or two small improvements.

For a start, this book needs a few large fold-out maps. When I was a boy, any book worth buying always had several large fold-out maps, usually of Upper Burma, showing railways and canals and things; and very useful they were, too.

It also needs an index. For instance, I tried to look up 'Gastritis', because I felt a touch of it coming on; but I couldn't find it on account of the total absence of an index. The same thing happened to my wife next day, only in her case it was dyspepsia.

There are several curious omissions in the text. Why, for example, are the first-class hockey fixtures for the coming season not listed? Why has no mention been made of the excellent work done by the Peat Moss Information League in parts of Rutland? And above all, why are there no footnotes?*

These imperfections aside, I commend this tiny volume to all philatelists and tree-surgeons, especially those with relatives in Sierra Leone.

LARSON E. WHIPSNADE

*This is the kind of footnote I mean.†
†You see how easy it is?‡
‡That's enough, let's not get carried away.

THE AUTHOR

Mystery still shrouds the true identity of Dirk Robson. At one time it was widely believed that the name concealed Dr Stanley Grunge, the former professional octopus-wrestler (now deceased). After that, scholarly opinion shifted towards Lady Flossy Strop-Fetlock; but when she accepted the position of honorary coach to the Burmese Rugby Union, this theory too had to be abandoned. It is now thought likely that Dirk Robson is really either Mr Chester Snavely, a jobbing gardener living in Limpley Groping, or Rear-Admiral Sir Shanklin Grapnel, R.N. (Retd.), of Peasedown St John. Attempts by researchers to gain further information have run into difficulties, as Mr Snavely attacks all visitors with his hoe, and the approaches to Admiral Grapnel's residence are mined. However, the publication soon of the first volume of a trilogy to be entitled *Dirk Robson — Man or Myth?* should throw some much-needed light on the whole subject, since it is said to have been written by Doris Flogg, the admiral's mulatto cook-housekeeper, who has been courting Snavely by post since 1936. Suggestions that Doris Flogg is really Dirk Robson have been referred to the director of Public prosecutions.

THE PHOTOGRAPHER

Collie N'Rose, the son of a pureblooded Watusi chieftain, is at present studying girls' legs at Bristle University. Like all the Watusi, he is eight feet tall, with extremely long arms; this enables him to shoot close-ups from long distance without using a telephoto lens. Collie N'Rose is a tireless photographer. One morning recently he got out of bed, caught sight of his right foot — and reached for his camera. After four hours intensive work, he was satisfied that he had captured his right foot on film. He put on his socks, and immediately saw the foot in a completely new light. Another four hours' work followed. He then put on his boots and once again was fascinated by the change. Finally, twelve hours after he had got up, he threw off his boots and socks and fell back into bed, completely exhausted. He is a chronically shy man and rather than speak to strangers will pretend to be a Norwegian seaman. He lives in fear of ever meeting a real Norwegian seaman, especially one who speaks Watusi and has two left feet.

THE PUBLISHERS

Today, two men spearhead the Mafia invasion of British publishing: Bugsy ('Boom-Boom') Schmelling and Lou ('Three-Fingers') Canelloni. Deported from the United States after being found in charge of a 64-seater bus which not only contained the bullet-riddled bodies of 64 of their underworld rivals but also had three worn tyres and a defective rear light, they brought their well-tried techniques of violence and extortion to the hitherto placid world of British books.

Of the two, Lou ('Three-Fingers') Canelloni is the thinker, the intellectual, the man who shapes the plans which Bugsy ('Boom-Boom') Schmelling — a 300-lb gorilla with a laugh like someone shaking a box of broken glass — then turns into action.

Their nicknames provide an insight to their characters. Canelloni got his as a result of using a booby-trapped typewriter, the gift of a business competitor who now decorates the bottom of New York's Hudson River, firmly anchored by a pair of concrete goloshes. That kind of thing could never happen to Schmelling. Illiterate, tone-deaf and colour-blind, Bugsy's only use for typewriters is to throw them at the heads of authors who fall behind in their writing schedules. When he found that his reputation was preceding him, and that writers were successfully ducking the flung machine, Bugsy — with a resourcefulness so typical of his unquenchable enthusiasm — carried with him a second typewriter, which invariably found its mark. This double-barrelled approach earned him the sobriquet 'Boom-Boom'.

The pair go together like assault and battery. It was Canelloni who dreamed up the idea of never printing less than half a million copies of any book, but it was Schmelling who overcame sales resistance in the trade by breaking three booksellers' arms in ten minutes. It was Lou's idea to price each book at ten pounds, but it was Bugsy who educated the bookshops into always paying him cash in advance, with the alternative of getting a firebomb through the fanlight. And while Three-Fingers must get the credit for suggesting that bookshops should cease dealing with all other publishers, Boom-Boom's persistence in chucking bricks through their windows really made this revolutionary scheme work. Their critics say that Schmelling and Canelloni are too advanced, too radical for British publishing; but they say it softly, very softly; and only to themselves.

PREFACE

This book is a sequel to SON OF BRISTLE, itself a sequel to KREK WAITER'S PEAK BRISTLE, which many critics hailed in 1970 as the finest load of old rubbish since Chaucer knocked the Venerable Bede off the top of the bestseller list in 1370.

Publication has not been easy. KREK WAITER'S was mistaken for a Greek phrase-book in Staple Hill (the Greek government hotly denied it) and for a toothbrush catalogue in Mangotsfield (the Bristle probably fooled them). Elsewhere, SON OF BRISTLE was displayed on shelves marked 'Baby Care' until Dr Spock took out an injunction, when it was moved to shelves marked 'Childhood Diseases'.

Nevertheless, and despite official intimidation – my work was constantly interrupted by the visits of unsmiling men disguised as postmen, gas-board inspectors, electric-meter readers and the like – I went ahead with BRISTLE RIDES AGAIN.

As usual, the critics have overlooked the best aspect of this book : its shape. It is exactly square. After you have read it – or better still, before – simply glue the pages together and you will have a comfortable, hardwearing floor-tile. At thirty-six books to the square yard, the cost works out at twelve pounds, excluding glue, which is far cheaper than using first-edition Chaucers, and also more resistant to heel-marks, soup-stains and a wide cross-section of childhood diseases.*

Dirk Robson
Bristle
October 1972

* Except croup, of course.

John Wesley, Broadmead

Queen Victoria, College Green

Temperance Permanent Building Society, Corn Street

Elizabethan Seaman, Council House, College Green

Samuel Plimsoll, Hotwells

Edmund Burke, M.P., Colston Avenue

Pediment, Victoria Rooms

Samuel Morley, M.P., Haymarket

Neptune, Broad Quay

Edward Colston, M.P., Colston Avenue

Edward VII, Victoria Rooms

William III, Queen Square

GLOSSARY

Many eminent scholars believe that the language of Bristle was at one time loosely linked to the English language, probably with a piece of string which broke under the strain. Today, Bristle is as distinct and unique as any of the other great modern tongues, such as Maori, Swahili, Choctaw or Scouse. The following glossary is a brief guide to some of the phrases found in this booklet. Further reading can be found in the standard textbook, *Krek Waiter's Peak Bristle*, while more serious students wishing to pursue the subject to 'A' level should acquire a copy of *Son of Bristle*. The publishers take no responsibility for loss of or damage to any reader's sanity. These booklets are not considered suitable for children under the age of eighteen months unless accompanied by an adult on the flugel horn. In exceptionally hot weather, a ukelele may be substituted for the flugel horn.

Aft Trawl: Considering everything.
Ark Tim: Listen to that.

Beers Port: Play fair.
Bell Tup: Who asked you?
Blood Yell: My goodness.
Blow Defy Know: Haven't got a clue.
Bomb: Rump.
Brassy Air: Underwear with uplift.

Car Key: Army brown.
Chuck Doubt: Expelled.
Corn Asian: Crowning.

Deaf Knit: Positive.
Dint Chew: Did you not?

Evil: Girl's name.

Fans Stress: Exotic costume.
Fine: Discover.
Flup: No room.
Forgots Ache: Kindly give me your undivided atten-
tion.

Ghost Ark Raven Mad: Behave oddly.

I Cadaver: It would be possible for me to have a.
Idle: Girl's name.

Lass: Final.
Leica Flash: Rapidly.
Less Fey Sit: We might as well accept the facts.
Less Packet Tin: I suggest we stop.

May Doubter: Constructed from.
Might Swell: For all the difference it makes.
Mike Cod: Goodness gracious me.
Mine Jew: Bear in mind.
Mint: Sixty seconds.
Miss Tree: Something unexplained.
Moat Wrist: Road user.

Nab Salute, A: A complete and utter.
Normal: Girl's name.

Nose Snot: On the contrary.
Now Daze: At present.
Numb Rate: Between 7 and 9.

Peace Ache, For: I say.
Phoney: I wish it were so.

Sarong Place: We should be elsewhere.
Scold: It's not hot.
Sink Ready Bull: I don't believe it.
Snow: You know.
Sod: How curious.
Star Tin Train: The fine weather has broken.
Summer: A particular place.
Summit: A particular thing.
Summon: A particular person.

Take Sages: It's not quick.
Tomb Mince: 120 seconds.
Tour Free: Less than 4.

Usure Red: Think about it.

Wake Sup: Give me a shake.
Wane: Hanging about.
Whirled A Good: Vast improvement.
Wide Jew: What were your reasons.
Wop Rices: How much is.

Yukon Talk: You're no better.

BOOK LIST

West Country & General Titles

WEST COUNTRY PLACE NAMES AND WHAT THEY MEAN by Cyril Davey – £1.50

LOCAL GHOSTS by M. Royal & I. Girvan – £1.95

BBC DAY OUT SERIES, 1, 2, 3, 4 by Derek Jones and Gwyn Richards – all at £1.50. With photographs

THE BRISTOL & BATH PUZZLER by Richard Palmer – 50p

LADIES' MILE by Victoria Hughes – £1.50

BATH PORTRAIT by Bryan Little – £3.25

INTO FRANCE WITH EASE by Helen Long – £1.95

SAFE HOUSES ARE DANGEROUS by Helen Long – £4.99

Quiz & Puzzle Books @ £2.95
Jane Austen by M. Lane
The Brontë Sisters by M. Lane
Shakespeare by M. Lane
Sherlock Holmes by N. Bartlett
Gilbert & Sullivan by N. Bartlett
Charles Dickens by M. Lane
Thomas Hardy by M. Lane

Language Glossaries @ £1.50
Rhyming Cockney Slang
American English
Scottish English
Australian English
Irish English
Yiddish English
Yorkshire English

A full list of Abson Books will be sent on request.

All available from booksellers or by adding 25p for the first copy and 15p per copy thereafter, for packing and postage from the publishers, Abson Books, Abson, Wick, Bristol BS15 5TT.